ruin			memory
leaves	and		water
paths	roads		tracks
the	capillary		ghost
a	pale		bird
grazing			air
the	sky	a	ladder

THE PALE LADDER

RICHARD SKELTON

SELECTED POEMS & TEXTS

(2009-14)

XYLEM BOOKS 2018

XY01 The Look Away (2018)
XY02 Field Notes (Volume One) (2018)
XY03 Heart of Winter (2018)
XY04 The Pale Ladder (2018)

Richard Skelton, *The Pale Ladder*, Selected Poems & Texts, 2009–2014
First published in 2016 by Corbel Stone Press
This edition copyright © Xylem Books 2018

Wolf Notes, The Flowering Rock, Typography of the Shore and
Wolfhou : The Absented Bield & Other Songs copyright ©
Autumn Richardson & Richard Skelton 2009–2013
Quoted material in the *Afterword* copyright © their respective authors
All other content copyright © Richard Skelton 2009–2014
The authors' moral rights have been asserted

ISBN: 978-1-9999718-3-0

Xylem Books is an imprint of Corbel Stone Press

FROM *Landings : Valley of the Small River* (2009)

3	Anglezarke
4	Colluding
5	Inventory
6	A Meadow Below Noon Hill Wood
7	The Grey Bird
8	The Book
9	Scar Tissue
10	Child
11	Coda
12	Something More Than Proximity
13	Lines of Flight
14	I Wanted to Tell You
15	Source
16	Hollow (Reprise)
17	Caged
18	Yield
19	Cling
20	Cuckoo
21	Seemed
22	Mirror
23	By the Banks of the Yarrow
24	Hordern Stoops
25	Firmament
26	Epitaph
27	Thing-Poems
28	Gone
29	Autumn
30	Fall
31	Mimesis
32	Made

33	On Samhain
34	River Song
35	Name
36	An Answer
37	Found
38	Remains
39	The Shape Leaves
40	Marks

FROM *Landings : Names. Dates. Genealogies.* (2011)

45	Abyss
46	Deserted
47	Façade
48	Miniature
49	The River Beneath
50	Feather
51	Root
52	Testimony
53	Line
54	Mere
55	Bond
56	Loom
57	Litany

FROM *Wolf Notes* (2010)

61	Ulpha Fell
62	Ulpha
63	The Unattended Stones
64	Proximity
65	Tenure

66	A List of Probable Grasses
67	Devoke Water
68	Cairns
69	Gift
70	On Naming
71	Place-Words
72	Formless
73	Echoes

FROM *The Flowering Rock* (2012)

77	By the Sea
78	Catch
79	Bell Stones
80	Succession
81	Sea Road
82	Beyond
83	Hills
84	Scailps
85	The Narrow Rooms
86	Corr Réisc
87	Seabhac Mara
88	Clamour
89	Departing

Moor Glisk (2012)

93	An Immense Morass Shut In Between the Sea On One Side and Mountains On the Other
110	Thig Taibhse Gu Dian an Àiridh
119	Notes on the Landscape
122	Errata

FROM *Limnology* (2012)

127	The River Before
130	Watering
132	River Song (1)
133	River Song (2)
134	River Song (3)
135	After the Thaw
141	From the Desert Waste
147	Imago

Single Poems & Small Collections (2009–12)

153	*Typography of the Shore*
160	Skin & Heather
161	Into the Bare Moorland
162	*Ridgelines*
164	Little Knives
165	Domain
173	Multitude
174	*Four Wing*
178	Rill
182	Rowk

Bark, Xylem (2013)

187	Saved
188	Founder's Song (Part One)
189	Lattice
190	Knot
191	Vessel
192	Shrill

193	Ladder
194	Skaych
195	Founder's Song (Part Two)
196	Follow
197	Let
199	An Inviolable Law

Single Poems & Small Collections (2013–14)

203	*Wolfhou : The Absented Bield & Other Songs*
213	Become a Ford
225	And the Dark Wheels Again
226	Evidence of Capillary Beauty Dismantled
228	*I Know Not Where*

End Matter

237	Afterword
241	Notes
249	Index
252	Place-Name Index
255	Bibliography

for Autumn

'... hold a light ...'

LANDINGS

VALLEY OF THE SMALL RIVER

EXCERPTS | 2009

ANGLEZARKE

A spur of eastern hills, 1,000 ft high projecting into the centre. The greater part a high moorland, 2,792 acres (167 of inland water). There is no village of Anglezarke, but a hamlet called White Coppice lies in the north-west, and another called Hempshaws in the south-east.

COLLUDING

Approaching this outcrop of trees, the atmosphere hits me forcibly. The pitiable nakedness of the boughs and branches. The sudden murmuring of the wind. *Colluding.* I want to make some kind of gesture. An offering. A mark of passing. And to leave it here. Tied to the land.

INVENTORY

How to begin writing this down? Shall it be a simple inventory? A list of parts. Names. Dates. Genealogies. Sound begetting sound. Endless melody.

A MEADOW BELOW NOON HILL WOOD

A sheep corpse lies near the fenced borders of a pine plantation. Just one of many I've seen in recent months. The eyes are gone. Always the eyes first. But what half-light breaks now, through those wretched hollows? What tenure now held in other places? Nearby, a body of metal fencing lies discarded in a rusted coil. Something more than proximity binds these things together. Perhaps when that fleshy corpse has long surrendered to the moor, this metal one will remain? A marker for something. An oblique form of testimony.

THE GREY BIRD

And there it is again. Distant, but powerful. A summoning call. Travelling the bank of black trees that points north-east towards Turton Heights. Across Hill Top and down Grange Brow. Circling this meadow. Drawing everything together.

Dark threads of song. Muscle. Blood. Bone. All towing the line at the threshold of something. A stark, two-note refrain, unaccompanied. Punctuating the silence. *Calling. Over and over.* Never answered. Removed from hope. And beyond dementia.

THE BOOK

And not just moor and woodland,
but the bones of old dwellings.
That somehow people thrived
here, once – perhaps a century
ago. Made these once-proud
monuments that now prostrate
themselves. Elbowing their way
into dirt.

And for some reason, shrouded
like the ruins themselves, an
anonymous archivist decided to
mark them down.

A private book of records.

Inventories.
Observations.
Epitaphs.

Type-written elegies from a
dimly lit past.

The date read 1936.

SCAR TISSUE

A woman in white stands just outside the entrance, hands on hips, head slightly cocked, looking squarely into the camera. A girl crouches beneath the window cradling an infant, almost receding into the wall itself. She looks downwards, as if expressing her reticence to be involved in this depiction of rustic domesticity. And last but not least, all but hidden by a wall, a young man stands, arms folded. A century's passing has since transformed this building from family dwelling into desolate ruin, home only to occasional wild birds and the sound of the breeze through the Yarrow vale. A century of collapse, decay and gradual surrender.

CHILD

From census and parish records:

SP, daughter of JP and EB, was born on _____ 1865 in Anglezarke. She appeared on the census on 2nd April 1871 in Anglezarke. The address was Lower Hempshaws Farm. On 2nd April 1871 she was a boarder in Anglezarke. She appeared on the census on 3rd April 1881 in Anglezarke. The address was Lower Hempshaws. On 3rd April 1881 she was a farm servant in Anglezarke. She died of drowning in a canal on _____ 1887 in Lancashire. She was buried in _____ 1887 in Rivington, Lancs. The address was Presbyterian Chapel.

More than these ghosts of buildings, the litter of sheep corpses, or the bones of grasses. More than skin and heather. Names. Dates. Genealogies. And this hovering, imagined presence.

And for some reason I think of Niépce's sun writing. Bitumen. Lavender oil. Pewter. Those first, eight hour exposures. The sun making a near-complete transit of the sky. Families of shadows. Acres of rest.

CODA

Along the borders, the high moors and unminded meadows. Mired in the earth and its green machinery. Meikle's forgotten children. As obsolete now as the flesh they disinherited. Chaff amongst chaff. Stunted. Leg-ironed. Bound to nothing.

But rattle their cages and something still stirs. A harrowed chorus resounds across the moors. Guttural coda to the song of a lost industry.

SOMETHING MORE THAN PROXIMITY

Will Narr, 1,175

Spitlers Edge, 1,286

Redmonds Edge, 1,230

Standing Stones Hill, 1,083

White Ledge Hill, 1,030

Counting Hill, 1,066

Black Hill Lower, 1,083

Round Loaf, 1,076

Black Hill Upper, 1,138

Great Hill, 1,250

Brown Hill, 1,030

Cold Within Hill. 919

LINES OF FLIGHT

I watch a solitary crow
follow the Yarrow upstream.
Tracing its own river in the sky.
Higher, much higher, gulls wheel
and meander, bicker and squabble.

Could I know the landscape
without ever seeing it?
Limn its ghost, mirrored
in these intangible paths –
these lines of flight?

I WANTED TO TELL YOU

I wanted to tell you about the river.
Its lymphatic grace. Its capillary beauty.
Devourer and devoured.
Predator and prey.

But the river is dumb to tell me.
These tricks of the light.
This grazing incidence.
A silvering prism.

SOURCE

To the source of the Yarrow.
Along the sheep tracks and broken walls.
Through the long grasses, the meadowsweet and the cuckoo spit.
If I spent enough time by its banks, could I get to know the river?
Its rapid tracts. Its sudden lulls.
Its changeling colour. Its constant cold.
If you placed me along its length, blindfolded, could I tell
you where, just from its sound?
Would that be enough?

HOLLOW (REPRISE)

False plane.
Hollow.
What caused
your loss of heart?

The dull
incessant roar.
Duress.
Commuted metal.

Sing
the air's engines.
Lichen
memory.

The sum
of all knowledge.
Withered.
Forgetting.

CAGED

Blood and the facial disc.
Noiseless. Unmoved.
A bright crest of optic nerve.
Against my dull eye and the hovering dark.

Keep watch the bruised horizon?
Watcher? You? Of fur, quill and bone?
Amongst the stone and fenced remnants.
Along the banks and the black fields.

Tiny palpitations. Filaments of life.
Hidden dramas of shade against shade.
And my senses are wretched. Caged.
Whilst you cage the sky.

YIELD

Come down by the banks of the river. Place your hands in the water. And hold them there. Slowly let the cold take you. Close your eyes and yield. And just as this river has found its way into the landscape, century over century. Find your hands and arms between rock and stone. Find your place through touch and instinct. And I promise that just before the pain becomes unbearable. Before your body begins to shake uncontrollably. A deep stillness will wash over you. And you will forget. And by the banks of the river. The pain will slowly, imperceptibly subside. The gift of stillness will gradually pass. And your muscles will move again.

CLING

Unrot. Cling. Withered, bloody inks. Phlegm and glimmer. She looks downwards. Centuries of the river's chatter. Tracing its perimeter. Phials of snow. Some kind of gesture. Families of shadows. Transits of the sky. Scenting the bones of grasses. Bowed, plucked, chafed. *Clamouring*.

CUCKOO

Who wrote Anglezarke?
The river, all mouth and
chatter, dries up. The
blabbing fields cry wolf.
Sheep stare blandly. In
the glib darkness I held
the moor in my hands.
Rolled it up in circles.
Conjured it from my
pillow. But now the
night eyes of the wood
glower. The moor turns
its back. Disowns me.
*You come here but we
don't need you. Begone,
cuckoo.*

SEEMED

it seemed to shake
to stir for a moment
(but for a moment)
and the sully of cloud
seemed to lift
from its back
and the sun

MIRROR

A lone foxglove grows between two collapsed roofing beams. Nettles gather around the blasted fireplace. Masonry lies covered in a lattice of lichen and moss. Beetles, ants and woodworm thrive in natural litter. Tiny specks of bright fungus trace contours along rotting timber. And as I follow these contours, they seem to recapitulate those of the surrounding hills. A grey mirror. A subtle echo. Question and answer. *You in me, and me in you.*

BY THE BANKS OF THE YARROW

the river's wound and
the staunching light

a reach of water and
night's inks

bleeding into
nothing

HORDERN STOOPS

A kestrel limns the vast banks of mist that coil around the lower slopes of Will Narr. Arrow. Rough hill. *Faierlokke*. The rowans are bearing fruit. Raspberry canes in the old garden. Migration differentials. The curlews are long gone, but swallows fatten themselves over the old hay meadow. I can hear voices by the masts of Winter Hill. Families of shadows on the moor. Bitumen. She died of drowning. A small, shallow dell.

FIRMAMENT

She was with me. We were walking down the old pathway. It was quiet and I heard her shallow intake of breath. She was looking up and I looked up. I saw nothing, and then I saw them. Hundreds, it seemed, high, high up in the firmament. They seemed to multiply before our eyes. The sky, sick with them. Metal. Burning. I felt her hand grip my arm, trembling, and tasted blood in my mouth.

EPITAPH

A girl crouches beneath the window. The bird slowly beats a track high above the water's edge. This earliest name describes the valley. Its shattered rooms. As if expressing her reticence. Along the banks and the black fields. I carry this river. And the offices of the dead. There is no village. Names. Dates. Genealogies. They cannot be contained. Fixed. Charted. A meagre epitaph. As I clamber over wood and stone.

THING-POEMS

Coil of barbed wire and string

Fragment of moss-fastened vertebrae

Thistle seed head and stalk

Bone of small animal

Mottled feather

Curved section of roof tile

GONE

The grey bird is gone. Its cry no longer frames the captive landscape. The curlews, gone. Their birthing halls deserted. The watcher, *aderyn corff*, is absent. Blended into nothing. Swifts, vanished. (In May, as I inched along Sheep House Lane in a violent gale, a swift rose up beside me, sails switching, seeming to share for a moment in my private struggle. Its arrow, I thought, had been blunted. Its scythe notched by the stony weather. But then it lurched forward, effortless, through a fissure of its own making, leaving me stranded, seasick, head reeling.)

And here by the path on Hoar Stones Brow, I find a large, black feather. *Crow rudder*. The only testimony – on this blank morning – that the air bore something on its back. Lifted high on its shoulders. Singing.

AUTUMN

A century's passing and the listening rattle. Crows bicker in the trees overhead. Rhymed leaves. Dew grass. Wing skirr. Engine. Siren. Machinic murmur. Threads across the river. Collective memory. Left to nettles and to barbed wire.

FALL

By Stronstrey Bank I watch birch leaves fall. Hurst Hill. Black Coppice. *Autumn's sickness*. And the old pathway, the grey stone and its glib markings. And the red road at dusk.

MIMESIS

There is a purpose here.
Following the bend
of this small, nameless
stream, my steps invoke
the path of the Yarrow,
miles away, as it tumbles
down from Will Narr.
Mimesis. The knots
of my hands and the
knuckles of ash above.
Joints. Junctures. Cross-
ings. An arboreal sweep
of collarbone. And
beyond the blood river.
A musculature of hill
and meadow.

MADE

Who made Anglezarke? I watch the wind-hover clutch the air above me. Does the bird stoop and kneel to the earth? (Countless times I've watched it fall from its ledge in the sky). Or does the earth, its play thing (that dull orb beneath it), rise to meet those open arms, like a child to its mother?

ON SAMHAIN

We are not on the old paths, by the road's edge or the boundary fields. There are no alignments, markers or signs. We are not amongst the sacred or the derelicted stones. No lights are fit for us, and we linger where we fell, or where fell things broke us. And although our tenure is passing, we are ever here, and ours is the moor, this shieling, this *ergh*. We watched the birthing of this river, and every night is a festival of the dead.

RIVER SONG

What have you given, that you have not already stolen? Flaunted desolation. Made your woe-songs in dull chambers, with dull strings. But our song is the river, the song of all deaths, the song of passings. At night you came, and we prepared a pathway down to the water's edge. But you clung to that which you must return, and lost yourself in the black fields. And now Autumn flounders and casts leaves into the swirling air. Will you ever return?

NAME

Though you are not here, and were never here, can you not feel it? Winter, calling each in, blithely gathering? Marking your place amongst us. Hill and bone. Skin and heather. A memory is nothing more than this. Nothing more than touch. Pressed forms in the cold, grey earth, and the river, ever yielding.

But these wrote words you hold against the circling seasons. Regret, loss, leavings. Marks on the skin. Unknow them. Listen, instead, to Winter's promise.

Come down by the banks of the river.
And I shall teach you the secret name of things.

AN ANSWER

And all the while
a voice, an answer,
rippling across the
moor:

Look, I carry this river
my hands are its banks
my arms its course
and I love.

FOUND

You passed me on the church road. Did you not see me?
Dusk. The engines. Your eyes. *Colluding*.
Last year I came here. Do you not remember?
They drowned this valley. She died. Drowning.
I found her in a handful of stones.
Do you think of me? Still?

REMAINS

but where will remains
these remains will

lasting in defiance
of the years

which fall
wingless on earth

THE SHAPE LEAVES

I turned and looked
for you becoming light

I turned and looked
for you becoming

and what impression
the shape leaves

MARKS

Footprints. In the soft, damp earth.
Mine encircling hers. How quickly
they faded into barely recognisable marks.
Had we really been here at all?

LANDINGS

NAMES. DATES. GENEALOGIES.

EXCERPTS | 2011

*I have heard
Strange voices in the evening wind; Strange forms
Dimly discovered throng'd the twilight air.*

ABYSS

I remember, in those first days, sitting on the high banks of the fledgling river. Staring out at the expanse of moor that seemed to stretch into infinity.

Aire leagte air saoghail dhorcha.

It seemed as if the earth
had tipped on its axis.
That the moor swung
teetering beneath me.
That if I didn't cling
to the grass banks,
I would fall
into an abyss.

DESERTED

Attend to me.
Field where vigils are held.
Grazier. Watcher.
Keeper of the valley.

Auðn, wilderness, desert.
Field parcels. Ploughshares.
Oxgangs of land.
A royal domain.

Auðnar-hús, auðnar-sel.
Observatory. House where
there is a corpse.
October 7th, 2007.

FAÇADE

From afar the moor is a façade.
A hanging of pale canopies:

>	*calico*
>	*muslin*
>	*hemp*

Rough cloths of muted grey,
yellow, green, brown. And
the sky a grey sheet.

But turn the corner
of the high lane above
Moses Cocker's and
the façade vanishes.
Wind-blown to nothing.

And in its place the vast,
looming earth.

And the river's yarn.

MINIATURE

The landscape is here in miniature.

Phials of soil. Brook water. Alluvium from the river.
Bark and fragments of bone, shrouded in muslin.
A small box of feathers. A trove of leaves and seeds.
Husks. Shells. Sheddings.

Each a vessel for memories.

This small pebble. *Godstone*.
Is between Hempshaws and Simms
on the path where the stonechat is calling.
December 23rd, 2007.

Ütic, ütic. Flint knap. A minute cacophony. Multiple tiny
reverberations. Colliding with the sound of my footsteps on the
rough ground. Chack. Scuff. Churr.

And as I touch this stone the bird is calling still.
Claghan-ny-gleiee. Remember us. Speak of us.

Arrange them on the map.
Place them according to where each was found.
So as not to forget.

THE RIVER BENEATH

There is a river
beneath the Yarrow.
This *other* is a dark
cascade. A black
and ceaseless torrent.
It is the lure
which all rivers
follow. And a line
that you can
never cross.

FEATHER

And
    the moor
            rests
on a kestrel's feather.

Brid – air-bride.

Thou thing that holds gravity.

I bore you on my shoulders. I carried you.

ROOT

A music hovers, gentle, over the valley.

Yarwe. Earwe. Yarewe.

The river is the root. The open string.
Old Rachel's a fourth. Simms a fifth.

And the path between them.
The most ancient of melodies.

TESTIMONY

The river is both hand and tongue
its testimony written voiced seen heard.

LINE

What line did the river first write in the valley?
What sense, made over and over, now senseless?

Dissolved salts. Glacial memories.
Inklings of maternal violence
written in moraines,
in alluvium,
in pulverised rock.

(A syllabary, loosened
from grit and clay.)

What is the true note deep within the foss,
heard, straining, above the froth and laughter?

An ancient, unchanging music
that scores valleys,
intones, beckons,
ushers them
into existence.

MERE

The reservoir is a mere dub in the river. The water
slacks, momentarily. Is skimmed for human consumption.
But
        it
                pushes
                      on-
                            wards,
                                        re-
                              doubling
                as it joins
           the black water,
dubh glaisi, du glais,
a swift arrow to the sea.

BOND

As the instrument has partaken
of the landscape – its body
bequeathed to soil, and later
exhumed –
so, a bond is made.

A pairing of movements. Of gestures.

The second finger hovers over the third fret.
The swift downwards stroke of the bow.
Kill note.

The string stopped with a feather touch.
A piercing cry.

And on the moor's edge
the red-brown bird takes up again.
Bridges the air above the Yarrow.
Its hunger momentarily sated.

LOOM

Loom house.
The farther gateway.
A small close
planted with trees.

A corruption
of Helmshaws.
A stone in the
left-hand side.

Shallow.
Incision.
The stone walls
are set.

There was a hamlet.
A.F. 1741.

LITANY

River –

*theaw'rt ith' clifts oth' rocks,
ith' huddin places oth' stairs,
le' me yer thy veighce;
for sweet is thy veighce.*

A murmur –

'twixt clack un chunner.

A litany of names.

Of those who lived and died
within its compass,
who left their mark on the landscape
or who were forgotten –
who passed by like ghosts.

Each, the same, made equal in death.

*Monny watters connot quench love,
noather con th' floods dreawn it.*

WOLF NOTES

EXCERPTS | 2010

ULPHA FELL

Stone folded into stone. Familial bonds.
Ice carvings. Water gatherings.
Worm shells. Brakes and mosses.

ULPHA

Wolfhou, [1279]

Ulfhou, [1337]

Ulpho, [1449]

Ulpha, [1625]

Ulfay, [1646]

Ulpha. [1777]

THE UNATTENDED STONES

A dark rain of ash above
grasses
fence the unattended stones
the tumbled wall
a path.

PROXIMITY

Sheer by *Brant Rake*
Quick by *Hare Gill*

Brush by *Storthes Gill*
Pale by *White Moss*

Ash by *Hesk Fell*
Dark by *Water Crag*

Shade by *Fox Bield*
Marked by *Gray Stone*

TENURE

Grasses, sedge and bracken
recover the rootless
felled expanses.

They break ground
for birch, for oak –

finding tenure in a
skin of soil.

A LIST OF PROBABLE GRASSES

Common Bent Grass *Agrostis tenuis*, Silvery Hair-grass *Aira caryophyllea*, Early Hair-grass *Aira praecox*, Sweet Vernal-grass *Anthoxanthum odoratum*, Fern Grass *Catapodium rigidum*, Blue Moor-grass *Sesleria caerulea*, Common Quaking-grass *Briza media*, Wavy Hair-grass *Deschampsia flexuosa*, Fine-leaved Sheep's Fescue *Festuca tenuifolia*, Brome Fescue *Vulpia bromoides*, Sheep's Fescue *Festuca ovina*, Strong Creeping Red Fescue *Festuca rubra rubra*, Annual Meadow-grass *Poa annua*, Tufted or Meadow Soft-grass *Holcus lanatus*, Purple Moor-grass *Molinia caerulea*, Mat-grass *Nardus stricta*, Smooth Meadow-grass *Poa pratensis*.

DEVOKE WATER

Duvokeswater, c. [1205]

Duuokwat, [1279]

Duffokiswatir, [c. 1280]

Devoke, [1626]

Dovic Water, [1769]

Devocke Water. [1860]

CAIRNS

Raised above *Devoke Water*.
Along *Water Crag*, *Pike How*
   and *Hall Beck*.

Scattered above *High Ground*.
Along *Ladder Crag*, *Rough Crag*
   and *White Wall*.

Left below *The Seat*.
Along *Sike Moss*, *Brown Rigg*
   and *Crosby Gill*.

GIFT

Where
the rowan grows through
touch, fissures become

becks rivulets gills

shimmed with light, as snow
gives way to sun.

ON NAMING

Gorse is the Ever-flower
    wedded to waste places.

Heather is the Brush-flower
    dry sea of violet.

Yew is the Stone-clasp
    reconciled to stone.

Bracken is the Red-wrack
    cast upon the fells.

PLACE-WORDS

Haugr, the grave mound, hill or heel
    Dim shape of rest.

Sker, the isolated rock, peak or cliff
    Broken face of grey.

Fjall, the mountain, height or moor
    High tumbling meadow.

Bekkr, the stream or little river
    Small rain in the narrow ravine.

FORMLESS

No voice but in the tongues
of others
no weight but in the pull
of mountains

> *placeless*
> *breath-stealer*
> *never dwelling*

a form less
clothed than air
tirelessly stitching-unstitching
hill side, moor and fell.

ECHOES

Harter Fell, a memory;
    the hill bereft of deer.

Birker Fell, an echo;
    the hill absented by birch.

Ulpha Fell, a reproach;
    the hill silenced of wolves.

THE FLOWERING ROCK

EXCERPTS | 2012

*From the water   they rise and fall
blue hills breathing   songs without words.*

BY THE SEA

Each morning
and the sounds of birds,

of wind
and water.

Each morning
and the ever-changing hues of the sea –

its manifold greys,
browns, greens and blues.

CATCH

The walls have vacancies,
interstices, vents –
they seem a pale net-work;
knots of grey rope
staked out to land
the great catch.

Those weir-men who
stitched them, laid them,
have long gone, down
within the hills' pores,
but whether by luck
or design the walls
stand still, whilst haw
and rowan heave and sigh,
catching the wind's
ceaseless expirations.

BELL STONES

Listen.
A low, muted,
bell-like sound.

They are *na clocha clingeacha* –
the ringing stones –
the bell stones.

Tread lightly.
Remember their voices
amongst the rocks.

SUCCESSION

First
        the hooked mouth
        of the sea
second
        the drill
        of the water
third
        the bleat
        of the heather
fourth
        the dwarf
        of the earth
fifth
        the head
        of the copse
sixth
        the cut-throat
        of the hedge
seventh
        the little singer
        of the willow
eighth
        the clacker
        of the gorse.

SEA ROAD

As the sea retreats
a way opens

to the blackened rocks
of an ancient and natural corridor.

The oldest, most enduring,
and yet most insubstantial road.

More ancient than bohreens,
than green roads, drove roads.

Commuted by heron, oystercatcher
and snipe. Forested by sea-oak.

Carpeted by red and green
and brown.

BEYOND

And beyond the shore

        ghost islets
                emerge,
          glimmer briefly,

then resubmerge –
revenants
of the waves.

HILLS

blue   grey   violet

       fissured   scarred   eroded

fluted   caved   porous

       rill-worn   costal   yielding

SCAILPS

Along the shattered pavement
are scailps (clefts, fissures, grikes) –
joints and seams prised open
over millennia –
the tireless work of water
(of acids and gravity)
as it flows
towards the
resurgent
stream.

THE NARROW ROOMS

Through narrow rooms,
along the small lengths
of stone corridors, passages, precincts

      birds   *glimmer*

alight on jutting tongues of stone
(from the open
mouths of rock fissures)
find resting chambers,
a moment's pause,
a brief dimming.

CORR RÉISC

Pulled along
unseen, familial lines,
the bird glides
heavily
with rigid, graceless wings.

Eventually it will ground,
this grey, silent kite.

It cannot endure on memory
and repulsion alone.

This shy bird is *corr réisc*,
the marsh bill,
but it could equally be called
an dealbh srutha,
the river statue,
or *an chloch a stánann*,
the gaze stone –
crouching, motionless,
on the furthest reaches of the boat cove.

But sometimes
it breaks its vow of silence –
a premonitory, piercing cry.

And then truly it earns the name
corr scréachóg,
or screech heron.

SEABHAC MARA

And further up the shore,
a white kestrel
hovers over the waters.
Seabhac mara.
A watcher of forms
beneath the blue-green
glass. A sudden diver
into the shifting tide.

Time after time
it makes a knot in the sky,
holding the fury
of the air at bay
with slow wing beats,
waiting
for a glint
of silver below.

CLAMOUR

There is a clamour
down by the sea.

Gulls congregate
on the narrow islets
just beyond the promontory.

Common,
black-headed,
lesser black-backed,
greater black-backed.

And mingled in
with the laridæn chatter –
the fraught piping of the curlew,
and the plaintive, solitary
calling of the oystercatcher.

Do they sense the downward cycle too?
The turn away from the sun.
The descent into autumn.

DEPARTING

Muich,
> sadness, dullness; a mist, a fog;

murchortha,
> things thrown ashore by the sea;

murdhuach,
> a mermaid, a sea-nymph;

murdhubhchaill,
> a cormorant (black sea hag);

murgabhal,
> an arm of the sea;

murmar,
> a murmur, noise of talk or of the sea;

murse,
> sea-shore, sea-marsh;

murthol,
> tide, flowing of the sea;

murthoradh,
> produce of the sea;

toichim,
> going, departing.

MOOR GLISK

2012

smoke land impervious sea
earth formed from black water
the ground a coating of thick light
a constant other

AN IMMENSE MORASS SHUT IN BETWEEN THE SEA ON ONE SIDE AND MOUNTAINS ON THE OTHER

a sector
of
vastness

wolf absence

wheat
flour
cotton

coal and water

a change cumulatively immense

this
the
curve
of
their
peak
and
decline

for more than a hundred years the land lay under grass

                                                old grey streets

'slenderly besett with eller, hasle and white thorn'

a series of rooms

        marshland scrub ling rough grass
sea-washed turf   pennine rock

the gaunt shelter of prehistoric trees

a slipper valley
                of
        rich alluvial milk

history can be traced
the figures can be broken down into
divisions
enclosure
agglomerations
boundary changes

    tracts of land   riven
                                    apart

                ploughing
                burning
                sowing
                harrowing

milk produced from burning timber

                        the forest yields   at day-
                                                                     break
      47,000 acres

the sky
                          harnessed
                                                        spun

agrarian roots ushered
a period of transition
a sudden excess
milk factories
plane the great body
field work
machinery
mortality rates

the rights of pasturage change hands quickly

underwoods thinned   the forest yields

disgorges

child labour

a hundred oaks   throwing off terrific heat

the voices have lost their old richness of dialect

the ash was hot   bright with new words

þyrne   holegn

elm   alor   wice

æsc   lind   askr

wicken   reynir   roan

berk   berc   beorc   birki

hæsl   aller   hæsel

ac   æsþe   *derwā

welig   wiþig

sealh   sawgh

sœppe

decade by decade
maps blurred
the loss of open fields
drainage schemes
inward movements
an unparalleled rate of increase
the nature of the soil
hedged and fenced
quarrying
woods felled
fields of drag
coprolites
blacksmiths
saddlers
root crops
drawn
measured

tame
        the woods of ash
                the roots of these yearnings

closed gates in the dales

        for a vast inland lake
        of black spit

branches of furze   clangour of curlew

            a drowning place

                      thousands went down

the cotton parade   a confusion of voices
a clatter of machinery

                the ravages
                      of men and fire
                the murmur
                      of women in the dawn

wrested from the soil

                                        'slenderly besett'

a variety of geological losses
nature's way of compensating
the gradient of this or that hill
fluctuating
exhaustion of the seams
the stream slowing down
stationary
feather-edged
a flint census
plough freight scattered
coalfields decline
a machine computing the rural exodus

Audley
Crowshaw Lodge
Spade Mill | Churn Clough
Alston | Dean Clough
Parsonage | Rishton
Mitchell's House
Fishmoor | Guide
Calf Hey | Ogden | Holden Wood
Rake Brook | Roddlesworth
Earnsdale | Sunnyhurst Hey
Ward's | Belmont | Delph
Springs | Dingle | Bryan Hey
Turton & Entwistle | Wayoh
Walves | Jumbles
Anglezarke | High Bullough
Upper Rivington | Yarrow
Lower Rivington
Worthington
High Rid

from seven million to nearly forty
           an insatiable thirst

strange new words in the chatter of mill girls
                              stunted and deformed

'I'd work but cannot – starve I may'

and the under-river
                  the great giver of all good

thrusting its head above a chain of man-made lakes
                                              graving

        'I have drawn until I have had my skin off me'

the drift from the land
wheelwrights structure the laws of migration
'it is often more difficult for a poor man to pass the artificial
boundary of a parish than an arm of the sea or a ridge of high
mountains'

blackened clothes of the moor
                cottons and coarse yarns
                    a hunting box
                          of
        peat grit coal loam
        one time under the water

its grey canopy reveals
        moss-stocks   hawpenny peat mosses
        traces of an old causeway
        from 800 to 1,400 feet above sea level

                fragments of curlew register
        and the retreating tide

'I am nobbut but a right little one and I never see the dayleet for weeks on end'

estuary marshes
        shut and salted

the rattle of a curlew
        under the loom

ditches and fortifications   bought and sold

                living traces
    of
extinct animals
        found in the dung of factory workers

                come then

    the day of the wolf

an increasing flood of trees
their fossilised beauty
buoyant

THIG TAIBHSE GU DIAN AN ÀIRIDH

I.   from one ruin to another

              dismantle   transform   become

                                        a ſþur
                            farm names
           an
       outcrop of trees

                    boughs and branches

the dark earth
                    drift
                                              heather
the black trees bank   half-forgotten
the moor beneath

the sounds cannot moor themselves

they ſþill   erase   a form of reticence

                    of ruin

     the recording
              like a map
                          lies

tender bark   a quarter of the heavens
to ſtoop   döggva
     to plunge   to bedew

something looks askance

                              a hawk skews

                  a bright light appearing under clouds

threads of a warp
a shred   hanks
    a fragment   of yarn

                  sweelin
                  sour-dock
                  keddle-dock
                  brushwood
                  (ſtunted)
                  devil's bit
                  dead tongue
                  moss-crop

all vanish

the channel of a river   wriðan:
denu: little valley   to writhe

provision in lands   the roof had fallen
mortar   porch ſtone
slab partition   fencing walls

                    fellon-wood
                       churn
                    cuckoo-spit
                    cuckoo-meat
                    ragged-robin
                      pissabed

all vanish

            the crow-gate   gata   road   guttural:

        various tracks form themselves into streams

crossing flows   ditches and other obstacles

              a   a deep
           channel   narrow
          for water   footway

                   properly interred

                      water-gait

                     procession
                      heretic
                     tradition
    a quarter of the heavens   birdcalls and traffic

    wish tokens   a shieling   matter
                                              substance
                                               essence
    all vanish

to reside
        in   the wind
a transient sight   a cleft or rift in a hill
                          locks of hair

north-west
                south-east

                          cordate

but there lies another   sudden   forgetting

the river
      branches
              gestures forcibly

                                outcrop   weight

              darkening its own making

rattle of leaf   flesh things
consequence   rapture

                            sounds begetting silence

the wreck of becoming
reluctant
mired in earth

disinherited

              a poverty of stones

11.   the moor wheels   turns   circles
                                                            disowns itself
     words fall   scattered   unceremoniously dumped

    they glower   collude
        shake themselves into new meanings

          sense conjured from chatter and darkness

    but in the end words fail
                      come up short   disperse

    the river   scenting their distress
                                              their fittingness
  makes a kill of their poverty
       choking them in its flood blossom

           decking the outside of dwellings with rotting flesh

           decaying in full view

  at night they huddle behind broken walls

  dead things   derelict   languishing
  yet fecund in their corpse foliage:
                               norse
                             brittonic
                                       crow food

and life begins again

                                new forms flower from clot litter

syllables   loan-words   root the earth

      feather themselves in greenness

                  rediscover sense

where there was none

swell   thrive

              pitch up fruit

                          make hay

and all the while

          the moor sings

gestures   encircling   firing the heather

the old argument   the old passion

      enduring

              despite the season

everything

      being subject to the same laws of flame and surrender

III. take up
        the stone
        the various tracks
               the streams
               ditches
                       mires

become
        rubble   heather
                sedge and moor grass
stranded
                              barely distinguishable
a glimmering thread
        half a mile upstream
                hemmed in
                              flecked with foam

place
        the stone amongst the others

shelter
        beneath the roots of old languages

                      remember
                         a
                      difficult
                      terrain
                     traversed

crossing streams confers immortality
the steep gully below

feeder conduits
overflow cascades

a liquid entity

                mark the map

                        a name for a place
        a shadow of undertow

                                bitter
                                and brittle

mirrored

                        ever seeing
      flight-limn   trace-paths   lymphatic

shivering

their names are lost
                all lost
                            ruin
                                      vanish

river flows worked the loom
disruption and transience
a legacy

fields flow directly from the river
reservoir   tap water   spires and columns

observe

        the water's impression

                        the mark of grasses

the sully of cloud left upon your skin

before

        you leave
imagine the former valley
impounded river water   dreams of escape

                if only the river had perfected itself earlier

before

        your body begins

                the muscles of the field

NOTES ON THE LANDSCAPE

West Pennine Moors: the early sources have not been exhaustively excerpted. A glacial effect on phonology. O.E. *ā* becomes *ō* south of the Ribble. Some names now lost with ground-nesting birds.

—

The wing of a curlew paid testimony to the early forms. Its call mimicking that of riven wood, adopted chiefly to illustrate dialect sound-changes.

—

The curve of its bill and the byht of a river, throwing light on the early history of the county. The pre-industrial landscape preserved in egg colours: greenish-dun to olive-green (blotched with dark brown and dark shades of green, thought to intimate early forms of writing).

—

Topography: dry grass, heather, unstressed and dialectical variants of rushes and sedges. Nests are often the junction of streams, shielings a depression in the ground.

—

The numerous names in *-ergh* and *-set* originally denote shielings. But many of these fledged at an early date.

—

Excavated borrans reveal word-hoards. Very few testify to a feeling for natural beauty, but there are many tree names.

—

Ash veneration is particularly frequent. Cf. an A.D. 854 charter:
> 'quendam fraxinum quem
> imperiti sacrum vocant'

(an ash-tree which the ignorant call holy). The beech does not occur.

—

Bolton-Le-Moors Par: the north part to a great extent consists of moorland. Trees were caught and tethered near settlements. Grey witchelms by Horwich. Oaks by Darwen. Willow by Withnell. It is improbable that bark should have been lost so early in all these names.

—

The fertility of upland soils may have fallen substantially by the Iron Age. Loss of phoneme structure and destruction of loan-words in organic horizons as a result of burning. Peaty gleyed podzols and acid brown earths are palatalised. Nasals frequently appear in the fossilised remains of bird song.

—

Settlements built upon rivers reflect the sound change *o* > *u* before *ng*, common in Lancashire dialects. Riverine and estuarine alluvium shows traces of discarded consonants. Land fringing upland is subject to word-flood, adversely affecting ground-nesting birds. River byhts often accumulate twite and skylark.

—

Other species fare more favourably. Sphagnum moss promotes the breeding of snipe, dunlin and plover. Elsewhere etymological surveys have revealed deep Brittonic deposits beneath Old Norse and Anglo-Saxon strata.

—

ERRATA

for path read contour
for stone wall read scree
for field read moor
for clearing read wood
for hill summit read wolf-haunt

LIMNOLOGY

EXCERPTS | 2012

what line did the river first write in the valley?
what sense, made over and over, now senseless?

THE RIVER BEFORE

    before
  the river
  was an eel
    before
    the river was ash
      before the river
      was clumps of ice
    before   the river
  was a leaping-place
before
the river
was salt
  before the river was
    rising
      before
  the river was acting
    before
    the
      river
      was burning
      before
        the river was
        rarely seen
          before
            the river was true
              before
      the river   was a murmur
       before
      the river was abiding in light
  before
  the river was   receding
    before the river was nimble
      before   the river was welting

```
                                            before
                                                    the river was lying in wait
                                            before
                                                        the
                                                        river
                                                                    was
                                                        boasting
                                                        before the
                                            river was a desert waste
                                before
                                the            river was
                            a hungry mouth
                    before
the river       was a knot in wood
                        before
                    the river was
                    still
        before
the
        river   was
                washed away
before
        the river was
                wantoning
                before
                the river was gravel
                        before the       river
                                    was buried
                        before
                the river was grief
                        before
                the
                        river
                                    was
                                    hollowed
                        out
```

                before
the river was consisting of nothing
before the river was meaning something else
            before
                        the river was impregnated
                                    before
                                    the river
                                    was a bleaching place
                                                before
                                    the river was a seething pool
                                                before
                                    the
                                    river was

            hearing voices
                        before
                                    the
            river   was
                                    as
                                                an
                                                            aa
                                    á
            eá   eá
                                    ar
                                    ab
                        o
a

WATERING

                rising
   damming
                  reaching
                 reaping
                           lying
                   breaking
                winding
          making
              keeping
                        curling
burning
  scouring
                        stepping
  dwelling
            forming
 branching
    spreading
                                 rilling
                     lulling
   crossing

        mourning
      blacking
                      winding
              meaning
               playing
     having
   rising
                 trifling
              raging
           falling
                   cunning
    ploughing
yawning
         washing
        issuing
                       wetting
  turning
                 jutting
    quartering
being

RIVER SONG (1)

the wearing
of water

small stones
falling

the sickle
of the current

swiftly
death-giving

RIVER SONG (2)

the river a moor

the moor a river

RIVER SONG (3)

ink
black drift

ridge of earth
pebble shoals

current surge

sinew
vein
bog channel

murmur

AFTER THE THAW

                after
       the thaw
                        the white crest
a snow-cursed memory
        glaciers   called north
               drawn
                              by a pack of wolves

a small divinity
              something between
                              man and spirit
          cursed
              the sluggish
              movement of the earth
          coughed   and
                had a vision
                        a form of prophecy

  a spark
        of small tongues
                centuries yawning
      ran
                          sudden
                     through the heather
            became   a blaze of fire
                    precipitous
      peat splendour
   blackening

moaning for the deaths to come
      the river   uncovered itself
                     curling around the hag chasm
         where the salmon lay hidden

                    saps lymph blood
                        moving
                        humming
                        flowing

and the sea called to the river
                the silent shore-birds
      deafened   by centuries of hunger
            heard its faint murmuring

              word spread of its plenty
                            legends of its fish fulness
    springing up like osiers

            reaping   the river harvest
                  was the great question
           an efflux   of discord   bubbling
    havoc   the only course of action

perhaps
    it was the heron
        cast out   solitary
            that first left the sea strand
    to find the fertile river

years   was its journey
            fifty or more travelling on foot
                    hardship   bordering on madness

but   in the last furrow
                it found the river
                    digging itself in
                                building a pebble dam

in a corner
                    the river
                                                    raging
                                                                put forth
                                a terrifying stream of melody

            but the heron   carried on against the torrent
                                        and tasting fish
                                                for the first time
                                                        was intoxicated

words   formed   in its beak
    magical
                            as a ripple on water
                                    fluent abounding
            a loud emanation
            a giant cry
                    lonely   wild   growing

and the sea   called back to it
        a thrum   of jetsam
                        and then came the tide
    running
        along
                    the heron path
                    a sea-stream
                                                of salt liquor

but
    unknown   to the heron
                                        by tasting fish
                the bird
                        had   given its spit
                                            to the river

                  and so
                              the river
                                          took that
                                                      wetness
                  and made
                        water
            to ease its flow of blood

the small divinity
        yawning
                observed the tide   advancing
                the river   flowing
                        the time of mingling was near

but   sudden
                        then
          a spark
                of small tongues   ran
                    through the heather
                                          a blaze of fire
                              precipitous
                burning
                      all
                      in its path
            the river
                boiling
                            the sea
                                    receding
                                          boiling
                        the whole earth
                  blackening
                            centuries

when the flames
        had run out
                the river
                        was a burn
                the sea
                      a desert

and the oracle
                              that small divinity
              mourning
                                          murmuring
                    shed
            some
        eye moistness
and
        gave
                the river
          a little
                      wetness again

and
        so the river
                made its journey
                              along the heron path
                  into the sea
                            at last

      the salmon
                          sequestered no more
                          set about spawning

so that
their issue
could
make their wandering way
to far-off places

and
the small divinity
took to lonely solitudes
his body steaming
his fancy in a ferment
and
became
an eel
or a waterfall
foaming
falling

FROM THE DESERT WASTE

1.

from the desert waste   I have come
    from that which is dead   I have come
        to look for the beginning   for certain death

between low and high water   a message spelled in alluvium

        'find the great bridle   the channel worn by light
        and scatter your host in the mountain flood'

by some means of divination   the seething stream
    will find   its boarding edge   spawn sent   returning
        and procure the dark path   to sruth glan gun truailleadh

II.

river   I hem the margins   scouring   the dialect of your incessant chattering
        the wildest recesses of   filth   dirt   mire
            rich with   word cascades   gutter knowledge   sources of prophecy

nerve vein ditch   hold forth your black vessel   as I spill   upstream
    make a sling of your current   to transport this hollowed-out body
        restless   worn   ebbing   its knot of energy   receding

III.

time and again   I surge and fall
rent from the waters
the black precipice   vomiting a curse   in old and sacred tongues

centuries of ardour   wild desire   now rage   tumult   confusion
a great outpouring   barbed   twisted   boiling

however will I ford this foaming torrent
and procure the dark path
to sruth glan gun truailleadh

IV.

river   your winding road is buried
          its course   is hid   from sight

is there a charm or bribe
          that will ink the eel path   through the tumult

guardian spirit   great water serpent
                    give strength   to bear   the miserable journey

v.

the passage
    contracts
  a narrow neck
      a cough   of shallows   scarcely
        branching   winding   eel deep

and I can hear   less far away
  the lulling voice   of sruth glan gun truailleadh

VI.

stream   little branch   root-joint
from the waste of ocean   I have come
    to make this rud
            a hollow   in which to spawn

                    and the waters will brim from bank to bank

here
    I will make begin   again
        smooth out   a gravel bed   or grave
        and   broken   wait the pouring out of faith

                        begin at the beginning   begin   be

                                                                   ca

                                                                    a

                                                                    a

IMAGO

that
    the river   flows
        downstream   is a trick
              of the light
          of gravity
              the salmon
              better knows
          its true course
like it
the river
    yearns
        unceasingly
    for the high places
        inching its way   towards
            ancestral
    birthing grounds

                                a nymph
                  each century
            it moults
            arteries thicken
    burrowing   a little deeper
    backing
        a little further
            into a hole
            of its own making
        and then
                                a subimago
                its wings
            near full formed
        its belly
    cavernous   empty
                its mouth
                    vestigial

                        and finally

                                                                an imago
                    for a day
            a brief moment
    of ecstasy
                                    it takes wing
                        climbs   hovers
                copulates   with the sun
                                                expires
                            showering the fells
                    with black eggs
                    that sink
                            into granite and snow

SINGLE POEMS

& SMALL COLLECTIONS

2009-12

from TYPOGRAPHY OF THE SHORE (2009)

shell casts in sand

empty presses

birds track salt lines in
tidal measures

    footnotes

    addenda

    marginal scrawl

bracketed between
strand and drift

struck through

by sea

at the margins of the sea
behind the drag of tide
fetched up – departed

    heaped broken reeds

    vertebral dregs

    clotted feathers

    bladderwrack and

    driftwood strands

    shards of mussel

    glass and wire

    skull of small bird –

    spine still clinging

    light limned around

    orphan pools

revenants

on the fossil shore

desiccated

remaindered

stricken

bleached

exposed

prone

etched

brittle

hallowed

fleeting

forgotten

ragged shoreline
spurred stems ascending
brome and fescue
wind-kerned grasses

    matted

    threshed

    bridled

    thefted

    winnowed

    burnished

and in the surface of the water
a corresponding shirr

for every hare's tail

its answer

SKIN & HEATHER (2010)

a threshold
a moment of transition

climb the small stile
gather the small stream

leaves and water
the constant polyphony

moors like scar tissue
skin and heather

ghosts of buildings
families of shadows

a fissure
a feather

a gradual surrender
to stones, dirt and grasses

receive the river
its sudden lulls

without weight
or consequence

forming
binding

dismantling
everything you ever knew

INTO THE BARE MOORLAND (2010)

into the bare moorland
unhindered
nature will remake
again

let the moorland
go to bracken
and others
will follow

furze and broom
they come after bracken
thriving
to make a richer soil

furze will reach outwards
dying at its heart
and into its remnants
rowan and birch will seed

they are edge trees
and in time will make
a place for oak and
ash and pine

let the moorland
go to bracken
and others
will follow

RIDGELINES (2011)

I.   BLACK COMBE

The great
black spur
that hangs
down from
Great Grassoms
from Swinside
and Thwaites Fell.
A gatherer
of animals
(throstle
horse
rabbit
swine
raven)
of crags
gills and
endless gray.
Time and again
during the long winter
I've watched
darkness bloom
over
its charcoal stroke
waiting
for the moment
when air and stone
when day and night
become indivisible.

II.   CAPPANAWALLA

The great
grey whale-back
that rises
breaching
the sea
by Gleninagh
its flanks
encrusted
with
blackthorn
thistle
fern
ivy.
I climbed it
once.
Sat breathless
on the pale lawn
of its summit
amongst flowers
blue and yellow.
Saw a squall
far out
over
Galway Bay
bringing
with it
the threat
of rain.

LITTLE KNIVES (2011)

If I sing
little knives
can you catch me?

If I rise
æsalon
will you come?

I am weary
blue hawk
and the sky is calling.

If I sing
death-wing
will you come?

DOMAIN (2012)

Again   it buoys the high air above Abbey Hill
glints its hover-colours   brown hawk yellow hawk
repeated in endless variation

having noted its absence these past three months
these brief moments are thrilling ecstatic
alive

blood hawk
bod-gaoithe
bodaire gaoithe
brown hawk
castrel
cefnlili goch
cenli coch
cenllif gocb
cenllit gocb
cidil cocb
clamhan ruadb
coystril
crecerelle
cres-hawk
creshawk
cresserelle
creyser

I stumble for words like a child-bird clutching at air
trembling falling

not quite ready for the hand's task
I can only point flap gesture

criodvan
cris-hauk
cristel-hawk
croman-luch
crysacc
cryssat
cryssoc
cudyll côch
cudyll y gwynt
curyll coch
darcan
dearcan
deargan
deargan alltraidh
deargan-allt
dbuaven
fabbcun

but it stays
rocking waiting   patient

tending lines   fisher on air's fine ledges
keeping the great blue vessel afloat
tirelessly dropping anchor   (securing air to earth).

Falco tinnunculus
fan-hawk
fan-wing
fan-winged hawk
fanner
fanner-hawk
field hawk
flapper
fleingall
flutterer
fly-in-gale
fuck-wind
furze kite
gabhar
gastrel
gastril
gellan goch

Seeing it here on the west coast
is like recovering sensation in a deadened limb

over the years
the bird has become part of my greater body
and its absence is noted like a loss of faculty
of sense   of feeling

and I am buoyed by its sudden presence

golan goaithe
gwepia
guibiar
guibir
guipa
guipai
guipia
hover-hawk
hoverhawk
jack-e-stop
jack-hawk
jacky-stop
kastrel
kastril
keel
keelie
keelie-hawk

but perhaps this coastline
this blackened rock   over which I walk daily
marks the natural limit of its domain
the boundary of its hunting ground
a threshold   a darkness –

should I too
turn my gaze away from the shifting sea
and towards the grey interior?

keely
keshrel
kestrel
kestril
kisstrill
kistrel
kite
kryssat
maalin
mouse-falcon
musbajoc
peep-hauk
peerie hauk
pilan
pocaire gaoithe
púicín gaoithe
querelle

And all the while names swoop at my skull
mobbing clamouring

wind-stroller
wind-sprite
wind-thorn

quercerble
red hawk
rock hawk
ruadhan aille
ruadhan alla
ruadhan-aille
ruadhan alla
scudi gaoth
seabhac bui
seabhac buidhe
Sparrow-hawk
Stainyel
Stanchel
Stanchil
Stand hawk
Standgale
Standhawk

names that in this other tongue
seem the very language of the birds

pocaire gaoithe
púicín gaoithe
bodaire gaoithe

stangal
stangall
staniel
stanair
staniel
stannel hawk
stanning-hawk
stanor
staynel
steingal
steingale
stone-falcon
stonegall
stonehawk
tweedler
tygry
tykery

but

thoughts steal you away from now   it says
leave names for the dead   the sleeping worming hiding things
leave names for songs elegies afterness

they're not for now
for the living.

vanner hawk
vuzzy-kite
willie-whip-the-wind
wind cuffer
wind fanner
wind sucker
wind-bibber
wind-bivver
wind-cuffer
wind-fanner
wind-baiffer
wind-hover
wind-hover hawk
wind-sucker
windbibber
windhover

MULTITUDE (2012)

the multitude
of all reeds and rushes
grow out of bounds

they belong
to the margins of lands
beyond the pastures

the space between

they are the fringe
of the low lands
the sign of streams

they grow tall
between you
and the near horizon

they etch
their sharp lines
upon the sky

only on them
the keen winds play
their dry music

FOUR WING (2012)

I.   of solitudes
      mountains
      snowfleck winter

        flocking south
        a low
        sweet song

        the larvæ of gnats
        seeds of grasses

        lies with feathers
        hair or down

11.   with lanes
        hedgerows
        golden-yellow

        lined with roots
        a bank
        dark deep

        a summer of song
        scribbling ſprinkling

        from topmoſt bright
        long drawn out

III.   on blood
of moors
deserted heather

crow of prey
on wing
pale brown

a darker of hares
small birds mottling

plaintive commoner
with beak of lead

IV.   of night
serrated
flying hidden

bringing back
a moth
ash-grey

clearings bracken
pistol uttered

vibrating wheel
a marbled churn

RILL (2012)

Rill
streamlet
small brook
(SKEAT)

We might equally use the words rivulet or runnel. Often too small to be featured on maps, they are rarely given individual names.

But there are words, descriptive of even the smallest things, if we care to look.

Runner
small stream
Strint
thin stream as of milk from the cow
Syre
gutter
sewer
Keld, kell
spring
(FERGUSON)

Smother
foam on the edge of a river when it is in flood
Speat
sudden flood in a river
Threeple, tripple
gentle sound made by a quick-flowing stream
(PREVOST)

In addition to these, drawn from the
Cumberland dialect, there are others, in
Anglo-Saxon, Icelandic, Gaelic, Irish and
Welsh, for example.

Ge-rípe
small stream rivulet
Hlýde
noisy brook
Mǽd-lacu
meadow-stream
(BOSWORTH / TOLLER)

Bekkjar-rysli
babbling stream
Lækjar-sitra
little brook
Rennsla
runnel
water-course
Sitra, sytra
little rippling stream
(VIGFUSSEN / CLEASBY)

Crion-allt
small rill
exhausted rill
stream nearly dried up by the sun's heat
stream that dries in summer
Caochan
stream so small as to be almost covered by the heather
(DWELLY)

Feadan
brook
runnel
streamlet
Sruthanach
full of streamlets
(O'REILLY)

Gofer
overflow of a well
rill
streamlet
Nennig
small brook streamlet
Rhewyn
drain
gutter
ditch
streamlet
(SPURRELL)

Perhaps these and others are apt to describe the myriad subtle watercourses that thread their way down from Ravens Crag towards Dunnerdale Beck? Skeat also uses the word *strippet* to characterise 'a very narrow stream' – and certainly many here are barely a hand's breadth wide, more noticeable for their sound than their appearance.

During the past autumn and winter many frequently overflowed – flattening their grass verges in the rush to claim the valley floor. And just as those well-worn channels swelled, so countless more appeared – temporary, fast flowing waters snaking through the fields below the fells after periods of heavy rain. Perhaps these were the first tracings of new rills as they limned the path of least resistance to lower ground?

Latch
an occasional watercourse a miry place
(DICKINSON)

ROWK (2012)

when the stream's ink
spills

when the beck's margin
breaks

when water
hands itself to air

rewrites hills
makes illegible the glyphs of trees

when the line of sky and earth
dissolves

you give it a name

as if you could bind
in a net of words

that which forsakes gravity

BARK, XYLEM

2013

touch the bark
that was your skin

SAVED

I have saved
these words for you
held them in my mouth
between tooth and tongue
thorn and branch
unvoiced until now
when they fall
wasted
but necessary
like leaves

FOUNDER'S SONG (PART ONE)

found
a line between trees

lent by the late sun's
branching light
read
between
black boughs

LATTICE

a wood
fencing the horizon
keeping the dark sky
within its meagre lattice
brooding over a mossed stone hollow
hidden to the world without

harts move between trees
between shades
mark sentry paths
from beech to beech
their individual shapes like family

life means knowing the difference
the outer and inner forms
the worth of things
oak gall canker urea and spittle
and autumn's rotten leavings

KNOT

by which door
will you make your entrance
how announce
your trespass?

your unwitting clamour
unnatural scent
precede you
screaming

      beneath

the mute articulations of stems and branches
leaf chatter ligneous murmurs
scripts of bark and leaf
and the heretic voicings of birds

      a knot of grammars

which you will never unravel

VESSEL

make a vessel
for the things
you have brought

a small depression
in the ground

return them
to the sanctity
of dirt

wash your hands
in the brook
that runs nearby

look back and try to remember
what marks this tree
from any other

and although you will forget

each spring a tide
of blue will come

to wash this wooded shore
of winter's bitter remnants

SHRILL

the wood does not object
does not reprove, censure
it stands for nothing
demands nothing
but what you can give

but what can you give?
your heat is not felt here
your touch transmits nothing
love fear shame are nothing

your quickness is too needlessly spent
your sharp mind blunted by bark, xylem

go back to your clamour
your glass and metal

shrill for us your small and haunted song

LADDER

for
the
climbing
larch
light
throws
down
its
pale
ladder

SKAYCH

beyond the wood's meander
a wanderer with nowhere left to go
far beyond whatever passes for a path
where whatever passes does so
beyond sight beyond mindfulness

there it lies, quiet
beneath the shelter of fallen limbs
a broken thing
waiting for the beaten coda

wood burr
long bill
low pheasant

dun-brown heart of the wood

footed to the leaves and the eternal shade
of an untold understory
head tucked beneath wing, vermicular

no more those strange barks and hisses
no more skaych and vessop
crok crok weet and ever silent

the wood rejoins with nothingness

FOUNDER'S SONG (PART TWO)

found
a way across fields

flocked from the flight
of restless birds
stalked
through
grasses

FOLLOW

follow the rill back up the channel
find the place where paths become streams
      where air and bracken are thin

observe the marks made by your trespass
      the broken stems the bruised leaves

allow the line of hills to come between you
      and resolve your contradictions

LET

> let the hazel
> thicket
> itself

>> become
>> dense
>> unfathomable

> let the willow
> fall
> out of line

>> divulge
>> grow in confidence

> let the ash
> stoop

>> grow carefree
>> with age

> let the bracken
> find a way in

>> take a chance
>> with the briar

> let the rowan
> quicken

>> make bright
>> among
>> hawthorn and elder

let the wood
absolve
the clearing

let the oak
forgive
the axe

let the nettle
sting
your skin into song

AN INVIOLABLE LAW

where
each one of us
breaks
is up-
rooted
cut or fallen
two will take our place
stronger more vital
branching forking
tirelessly
mending

SINGLE POEMS

& SMALL COLLECTIONS

2013–14

WOLFHOU : THE ABSENTED BIELD
& OTHER SONGS (2013)

touch path
slope stirs
from memory
into carvings

1279
Duuokwat:
ice wolves. fells felled. filament rain.
seed memory. brythonic mosses.

Haugr:
cold cast
above meadow grass
rough grave
left to heather

1337
Birker:
where are the birch gatherings?
the fell oak expanses?

pale saps
seeds
rest in grasses
wolf barren

1449
Harter:
how is the deer rake left unattended?

dry
ravine
revenant path
to the sea

1695
Uffay:
the hill is echoless of wolves.
the brant earth silenced
of yew tongues.

1769
the fell wall stirs. muscles a rough way upwards.
tirelessly weights the waste. grows grey.
skins birch, rowan, heather.
seeks wolves.

1860
into the absented bield. the hill grave.
recover within fox memory. moss drifts.
brush soils last shaped by bracken.
worm ground. familial earth. ready.

BECOME A FORD (2013)

beingblackin
gbranchingbr
eakingburnin
gcrossingcun
ningcurlingd
ammingdwelli
ngfallingfor
minghavingis
suingjutting
keepinglulli
nglyingmakin
gmeaningmour
ningplayingp
loughingquar
teringraging
reachingreap
ingrillingri
singscouring
spreadingste
ppingtriflin
gturningwash
ingwettingwi
ndingyawning

b e

c   o

m   e

                        a   f o r

                                d

        c h
    a   n

        n   e l

                                    o r

                        g   u t t
              e

                                    r

ming   li
ng

          m
              a

  k   i n g
                        n
       e

                  w

p

o

u

r

i n g

f

a i
t
h

a

w
a

y

w

i

t

h

g
r

a

v
i

t

y

AND THE DARK WHEELS AGAIN (2013)

and the dark wheels again
winding round
a line drawn straight up
a line of beauty
up into the heights
and on those winding circles
(wide wings outstretched
no beat or flutter
nothing tangible
to rest his tail against)
up goes the hawk
round and round

EVIDENCE OF CAPILLARY BEAUTY DISMANTLED (2014)

dull brown earth
its veil of vegetation
a rub of greenness
held in measure
given word
and each word its perimeter
its fold
stake or pasture
fixed and charted
(edge folded on itself
impenetrable)

from nameless to name
to nameless again
in time

all is gone
all is left

the land endures
itself
breeding green
from brown

mending paths
footprints absolved
(their tenure always passing)

and something returns
that which was deferred
held suspended
dammed now flooding

a spur
transformed

and the sound of crows

I KNOW NOT WHERE (2014)

Walked
the twisting tracks
the hollow roads:

fringed
with small life

Walked
by the black brook:

the veil of life
obscured
morning and evening

Walked
the palest current:

a half-marked
glittering
crescent stream

Walked
until dark returned:

found under
gaunt flowers

Walked
through air:

a ceaseless lark winding
green songs of the dead

Walked
by furze spinning
a thin, strange brook:

perpetual murmur

Walked
alone:

adders-tongue
low ferns
advances of stitchwort
found under trees

Walked
the invisible veil:

the shadows of oaks
a blackened murmur

Walked
with ivy
twisting
bristled serpents:

dark laden

Walked
where
noise flowers
in multitudes:

plentiful

AFTERWORD

The Pale Ladder collects together the majority of Richard Skelton's poetic writing published between 2009 and 2014, including work co-authored with Autumn Richardson – an endeavour that must surely constitute one of the most sustained and significant small press collaborations of recent years.

Over one hundred poems and texts are reprinted in *The Pale Ladder*, including work from many long out-of-print and limited edition titles such as *Flock*, *Sightings* and *Become a Ford*. With the exception of the latter, notable omissions are the more visually oriented pieces from Skelton's oeuvre, as epitomised by the *grid-poems* of *Landings* (2009), and the *tree cross-sections* of *Relics* (2013). These and others may provide the focus for a later companion volume.

In gathering these various works together for the first time, it is possible to glimpse the artist's overarching themes – the interconnecting threads – and to plot their development. Key among them is the desire to observe, to bear witness and to record the testimony of the land itself, through its many and varied agencies – its topography and weather, its flora and fauna, its place-names and dialects, and its records and archives. Martyn Hudson describes this as 'a sustained reflection on the nature of land and biography' – an 'idiosyncratic archiving of local topographies and the secrets they hold'.[1] Crucially, he identifies Skelton's focus on the 'borders between the human and the non-human, and between actuality and imagination', and it is this attention to what lies beyond material reality that characterises much of Skelton's work – his willingness to give voice to the countless *others*; the land's heretical and supernatural voices:

> Who wrote Anglezarke?
> The river, all mouth and
> chatter, dries up. The
> blabbing fields cry wolf.
> Sheep stare blandly. In
> the glib darkness I held
> the moor in my hands.
> Rolled it up in circles.
> Conjured it from my
> pillow. But now the
> night eyes of the wood
> glower. The moor turns
> its back. Disowns me.
> *You come here but we*
> *don't need you. Begone,*
> *cuckoo.*
>
> —(*Cuckoo*, 2009)

The various testimonies 'documented' here are, as Robert Macfarlane observes, 'litanies spoken against loss',[2] and this archival function of the *word-hoard* is a deep imperative running through much of the writing published in *The Pale Ladder*. The act of naming – as a means, not of possessing things, but of simply acknowledging their existence – is a powerful facility of language, but Skelton consistently challenges it by drawing attention to where language – or at least *our* language – falls short:

```
the moor wheels     turns    circles
                             disowns itself
    words fall     scattered   unceremoniously dumped
```

they glower   collude
    shake themselves into new meanings

    sense conjured from chatter and darkness

but in the end words fail
                come up short   disperse

—(from *Thig Taibhse Gu Dian An Àiridh*, 2012)

the mute articulations of stems and branches
leaf chatter ligneous murmurs
scripts of bark and leaf
and the heretic voicings of birds

        a knot of grammars

which you will never unravel

—(from *Knot*, 2013)

But despite this, Skelton returns again and again to the incantatory rhythm of the litany – all grammar and superfluous vocabulary falls away to reveal the simplest, perhaps most primal, thread of language itself: the list. As Macfarlane notes in his comparison to the figure from Finnish mythology, Skelton's is a writing that 'longs for that power of utterance also sought by Vainamoinen: the magic words'.

1. Martyn Hudson, 'Archive, Sound and Landscape in Richard Skelton's Landings Sequence', *Landscapes Journal*, Volume 16, Number 1, 2015, pp. 66-7.
2. Robert Macfarlane, *Landmarks*, Hamish Hamilton, 2015, p. 183.

NOTES

1. VALLEY OF THE SMALL RIVER : First published in *Landings*, 2009, Sustain-Release Private Press.
3. ANGLEZARKE : An area of the West Pennine Moors in northern England. *Landings* is a collection of texts concerning this landscape drawn from various sources, including historical treatises, maps, parish records, census data and the author's own notes. This excerpt is adapted from *The Victoria History of the County of Lancaster, Volume V*, 1911.
5. INVENTORY : Excerpted from an original text entitled *The Copse at the Brow of School House Lane*.
8. THE BOOK : The 'book' itself is an anonymous, loose-leaf collection of texts about local history, and specifically the ruined farmhouses on Anglezarke and Rivington Moor.
9. SCAR TISSUE : Excerpted from the original. The Yarrow, a fledgling river born on the hill slopes of Will Narr, features prominently in *Landings*.
19. CLING : *Landings* is not only drawn from a variety of sources, but many of its texts are reassemblings of the same raw material. The phrase 'some kind of gesture', for example, is repeated from *Colluding*.
24. HORDERN STOOPS : *Faierlokke*, an old name for Rivington Pike, a hill-summit on Rivington Moor.
27. THING POEMS : Excerpted from an original text entitled *Pariah*.
28. GONE : *Aderyn corff*, 'corpse bird' in the Welsh language, is a folk-name for the barn owl, *Tyto alba*. The 'watcher' of the poem *Caged*.
33. ON SAMHAIN : *Ergh*, a Middle-English variant of *erg*, 'a shieling'.
43. NAMES. DATES. GENEALOGIES. : First published in the 3rd Edition of *Landings*, 2011, Sustain-Release Private Press.

'I have heard / Strange voices' quoted from *Joan of Arc* by Robert Southey.

45. ABYSS : *Aire leagte air saoghail dhorcha*, 'his thoughts fixed on worlds unknown', found in *A Gaelic Dictionary in Two Parts* by Robert Armstrong.

46. DESERTED : *Auðn*, 'deserted', auðnar-hús, 'deserted huts', auðnar-sel, 'deserted shielings', found in *An Icelandic-English Dictionary* by Gudbrand Vigfusson.

48. MINIATURE : *Ütic*, W. Percival Westell's description of the stonechat's call, in his book, *British Nesting Birds*; *Claghan-ny-gleiee*, 'a stonechat', from *The Manx Dictionary in Two Parts* by John Kelly.

50. FEATHER : *Brid*, 'a bird', found in *A Glossary of the Lancashire Dialect* by John H. Nodal and George Milner.

51. ROOT : *Yarwe. Earwe. Yarewe.*, a partial toponymic sequence for the River Yarrow.

54. MERE : *Dub*, a dialect word for a pool, or deep place in a river, of possible Gaelic origin; *the black water, dubh glaisi, du glais*, a reference to the River Douglas; *swift arrow*, a reference to the River Ribble, with which the Douglas eventually merges: 'Rhe, a root found in many languages, meaning swift, or to run. The names of many rivers, as Rea, Rye, Rey, Ribble, &c., are derived from it', found in *The Survey Gazetteer of the British Isles* by J.G. Bartholomew.

55. BOND : *Instrument*, a reference to the artist's practice of burying small musical instruments in the soil and later exhuming them.

57. LITANY : *Theaw'rt ith' clifts oth' rocks* and *Monny watters connot quench love*, both quoted from *The Song of Solomon in the Lancashire Dialect* by James Taylor Staton.

59. WOLF NOTES : Written with Autumn Richardson. First published by Corbel Stone Press, 2010, in a very limited

'folio' edition with supplementary texts. All texts were originally numbered but otherwise untitled.

62. ULPHA : A partial toponymic sequence for the place-name 'Ulpha'. *Wolf Notes* is written for the upland landscape between the Duddon Valley and Eskdale, Cumbria, England, which includes an area known as Ulpha Fell. The place-name is Old Norse in origin, and is thought to mean 'hill of the wolf' or 'hill of the man known as Ulf'.

67. DEVOKE WATER : A partial toponymic sequence for the place-name 'Devoke Water', which is thought to be of early British origin, meaning 'the black one'.

75. THE FLOWERING ROCK : Written with Autumn Richardson for the landscape around Ballyconry, County Clare, Ireland. First published in *Field Notes (Volume One)*, Corbel Stone Press, 2012, ISBN 978-0-9572121-0-7. All texts originally appeared untitled. Thanks to Caoimhín MacGiolla Léith for providing the Irish translations.

86. CORR RÉISC : A common Irish name for the grey heron, which translates as 'marsh bill'. Both *river statue* and *gaze stone* are coinages; *Corr scréachóg*, 'screech heron', is curiously enough a folk-name for the screech- or barn-owl, found in Dinneen's dictionary, which also mentions *corr scéacha, corr scréadóige* and simply *scréachóg*. Here *corr scréachóg* has been reappropriated for the heron.

87. SEABHAC MARA : Irish for 'sea hawk'. This, and *white kestrel*, are coinages for an unknown bird of the gull family, seen fishing just off the shore by Ballyconry.

91. MOOR GLISK : First published by Corbel Stone Press, 2012, ISBN 978-0-9572121-2-1. A continuation and reassembling of *Landings*, retelling the history of the county of Lancashire, England, and drawing on such texts as *It's an Old Lancashire Custom* by Sylvia Lovat Corbridge; *Soils of the British Isles* by

L.F. Curtis, F.M. Courtney and S. Trudgill; *The Place-Names of Lancashire* by Eilert Ekwall, and *Rural Depopulation in England and Wales* by John Saville.

93. AN IMMENSE MORASS : M. Léonce de Lavergne described Lancashire in 1854 as 'an immense morass, shut in between the sea on one side and mountains on the other; stiff clay land, with an impervious subsoil everywhere hostile to farming; add to this a most gloomy climate, continual rain, a constant cold sea-wind, besides a thick smoke shutting out what little light penetrates the foggy atmosphere; and lastly, the ground, the inhabitants, and their dwellings completely covered with a coating of black dust, – fancy all this, and some idea may be formed of this strange county, where the air and the earth seem only one mixture of coal and water!'

104. AN IMMENSE MORASS : *Audley, etc*, a list of reservoirs on Lancashire's West Pennine Moors.

110. THIG TAIBHSE GU DIAN AN AIRIDH : 'Ghosts shall issue wildly from the osier meadow', found in *A Gaelic Dictionary in Two Parts* by Robert Armstrong, and first quoted in *Landings*.

122. ERRATA : Originally included as an errata note within *Moor Glisk*, but addressing 'errors' in the landscape, rather than the text itself.

125. LIMNOLOGY : First published by Corbel Stone Press, 2012, ISBN 978-0-9572121-3-8. All texts originally appeared untitled. *The River Before*, *Watering*, *After the Thaw* and *From the Desert Waste* were assembled from a corpus of over 1,000 'water-words' and their definitions.

127. THE RIVER BEFORE : The poem ends with a list of ancient water words – *as* (Irish) 'a waterfall'; *an* (Manx) 'water'; *á* (Old Icelandic) 'a river'; *aa* (Manx) 'a ford'; *eá* (Anglo-Saxon) 'a river'; *ar* (Manx) 'water', 'a collection of water'; *ab* (Old

Irish) 'a river'; *o* (Manx) 'a pouring out of water'; *a* (Manx) 'a ford'.

141. FROM THE DESERT WASTE : *Sruth glan gun truailleadh*, 'a stream pure and undefiled', found in *A Gaelic-English Dictionary* by Edward Dwelly.

153. TYPOGRAPHY OF THE SHORE : Written with Autumn Richardson for Tentsmuir beach, Scotland. First published by Corbel Stone Press, 2009.

160. SKIN AND HEATHER : First published by Corbel Stone Press, 2010. Text assembled from *Landings*.

161. INTO THE BARE MOORLAND : First published by Corbel Stone Press, 2010. Adapted from *The Permaculture Way* by Graham Bell.

162. RIDGELINES : First published by Corbel Stone Press, 2011.

164. LITTLE KNIVES : Previously unpublished.

165. DOMAIN : First published by Corbel Stone Press, 2012. Kestrel (*Falco tinnunculus*) populations in the United Kingdom have declined for many years. The reasons are as yet unknown, but habitat loss is thought to be a key factor. *Domain* is a poem about the sighting of a kestrel on the west coast of Ireland. It hovers over a landscape composed of words for the bird in various dialects and languages. These names, including those in English, Welsh, Irish and Gaelic, are something of a linguistic population count. By no means complete, the list represents a historical, rather than contemporary, survey – a form of salvage, a shoring up, an attempt to stem the tide. *Wind-stroller, wind-sprite* and *wind-thorn* are English translations of the Irish *pocaire gaoithe, púicín gaoithe* and *bodaire gaoithe*. Some license has been used in deriving *wind-thorn*, as *bodaire gaoithe* literally translates as *wind-prick*, or *wind-penis*, meaning, 'bird that copulates with the air'. This term is perhaps not entirely

idiomatic to Irish, as there is also an English north country folk-name, *fuck-wind* – which seems self-evident enough, except that it may derive from the Old Norse *fjuka*, 'being tossed or driven by the wind'.

173. MULTITUDE : First published by Corbel Stone Press, 2012. Text assembled from *Rushes and Reeds* by Alice Meynell.

174. FOUR WING : First published by Corbel Stone Press, 2012. Texts assembled from *British Nesting Birds* by W. Percival Westell.

178. RILL : First published by Corbel Stone Press, 2012.

182. ROWK : First published by Corbel Stone Press, 2012, as part of the *Flock* limited boxed edition.

185. BARK, XYLEM : First published by Corbel Stone Press, 2013.

194. SKAYCH : *Skaych, vessop, crok, weet*, words used by W. Percival Westell, in his *British Nesting Birds*, to describe the call of the woodcock.

203. WOLFHOU : Written with Autumn Richardson. First published by Corbel Stone Press, 2013. Text assembled from *Wolf Notes*.

204. WOLFHOU : *Duuokwat*, an historic place-name for Devoke Water.

205. WOLFHOU : *Haugr*, an Old Norse word found in place-names and the Cumbrian dialect as *howe* or *how*, 'a hill or grave mound'.

206. WOLFHOU : *Birker*, a place-name derived from the Old Norse, 'shieling by the birch trees'.

208. WOLFHOU : *Harter*, a place-name derived in part from the Old Norse for 'hart or stag'; *rake*, Cumbrian dialect, 'a path'.

210. WOLFHOU : *Uffay*, an historic place-name for Ulpha.

213. BECOME A FORD : First published by Artist's Editions (an imprint of Corbel Stone Press), 2013. A continuation of *Limnology*. 38 'ings' taken from dictionary definitions of

'water-words', arranged in a grid and used as a source to form a new text work.

225. AND THE DARK WHEELS AGAIN : Previously unpublished. Assembled from *Birds Climbing the Air* by Richard Jefferies.

226. EVIDENCE OF CAPILLARY BEAUTY DISMANTLED : First published by Corbel Stone Press, 2014, as part of the *Sightings* special edition. Text assembled from *Landings*.

228. I KNOW NOT WHERE : First published by Corbel Stone Press, 2014. Ten *word-paths* through the writing of Dorothy Wordsworth. Many of the entries from Dorothy's Alfoxden journal start with the word *walked*, before departing, linguistically and geographically. In particular, her phrase 'walked I know not where' (the only entry for the 30th of March, 1798), is positively enigmatic – it seems to invite reverie, to solicit a kind of wayward revisiting of her own textual landscape. Commissioned by The Wordsworth Trust as part of the *Wordsworth and Bashō : Walking Poets* exhibition.

INDEX

Air, Sky   10, 13, 16, 17, 19, 25, 28, 32, 34, 44, 47, 50, 55,
                            72, 87, 96, 113, 162, 164, 165, 166, 167, 173, 182,
                            189, 196, 230

Birds   7, 9, 13, 17, 20, 24, 26, 28, 29, 32, 48, 50, 55,
                            77, 80, 81, 85, 86, 87, 88, 89, 101, 107, 108, 111,
                            112, 114, 119, 121, 136, 137–9, 154, 156, 162, 164,
                            165–172, 174–177, 190, 194, 195, 225, 227, 230

Blood   7, 17, 19, 25, 31, 136, 138, 165, 176

Bone   7, 8, 10, 17, 19, 27, 31, 35, 35, 48

Bracken   65, 70, 161, 177, 196, 197, 212

Corpses, Death   6, 10, 26, 33, 34, 46, 57, 114, 132, 135, 141–6,
                            164, 172, 230

Dark, Night   7, 17, 20, 23, 33, 34, 49, 63, 64, 110, 113, 114,
                            119, 141, 143, 162, 169, 175, 176, 177, 189, 225,
                            229, 232

Dirt, Earth, Soil   8, 11, 32, 35, 38, 40, 45, 47, 48, 55, 65, 80, 92,
                            100, 102, 110, 113, 115, 121, 134, 135, 138, 142,
                            160, 161, 167, 182, 191, 210, 212, 226

Fields, Meadows   6, 7, 11, 15, 17, 20, 24, 26, 31, 33, 34, 46, 66, 71,
                            97, 100, 117, 118, 122, 179, 181, 195, 205

Grasses   10, 15, 19, 29, 45, 63, 65, 66, 94, 116, 118, 119,
                            158, 160, 162, 174, 181, 195, 205, 207

Heather	10, 35, 70, 80, 110, 115, 116, 119, 135, 138, 160, 176, 179, 205, 211
Hills	3, 6, 7, 12, 22, 24, 30, 31, 35, 71, 72, 73, 78, 83, 103, 113, 122, 165, 182, 196, 203, 210, 212
Kestrel, Wind-hover	24, 32, 50, 55, 87, 165–172
Language, Names, Words	5, 10, 12, 26, 31, 35, 43, 57, 62, 64, 66, 67, 68, 71, 73, 86, 87, 89, 98, 99, 104, 105, 110, 114–5, 116, 117, 119–121, 136, 137, 141–6, 162–3, 165–172, 178–181, 182, 187, 194, 204, 205, 206, 208, 210, 226
Marks	4, 6, 8, 30, 33, 35, 40, 57, 64, 117, 118, 169, 189, 191, 196, 229
Moor	3, 6, 8, 11, 20, 24, 33, 36, 45, 47, 50, 55, 66, 71, 72, 91–122, 133, 160, 161, 176
Music, Song, Sound	5, 7, 9, 11, 13, 14, 32, 34, 49, 51, 53, 75, 77, 84, 86, 87, 100, 108, 110, 113, 115, 119, 121, 132–4, 135–7, 170–2, 173, 174–7, 188, 190, 192, 195, 198, 203, 227, 230–2
Paths, Roads, Tracks	13, 15, 25, 26, 28, 30, 31, 33, 34, 37, 48, 51, 63, 81, 112, 116, 117, 122, 137–9, 141–146, 154, 181, 189, 194, 196, 203, 209, 227, 228–232

Rivers, Streams, Water	3, 13, 14, 15, 18, 19, 20, 23, 26, 29, 31, 33, 34, 35, 36, 45, 47, 48, 49, 51, 52, 53, 54, 57, 61, 64, 67, 68, 71, 77, 80, 81, 84, 86, 87, 92, 93, 103, 105, 107, 111, 112, 113, 114, 116, 117, 118, 119, 121, 125–148, 158, 160, 173, 178–181, 182, 191, 196, 213–224, 229, 230
Rock, Stone	12, 17, 18, 26, 28, 30, 30, 33, 37, 48, 53, 56, 57, 61, 63, 64, 70, 71, 75–89, 94, 111, 113, 116, 122, 132, 160, 162, 169, 170, 171, 189
Ruins	8, 9, 10, 22, 26, 33, 37, 38, 48, 51, 56, 63, 110, 117
Sea, Shore	54, 70, 77, 80, 81, 82, 84, 87, 88, 89, 92, 93, 94, 106, 107, 136–9, 153–9, 163, 169, 209
Branches, Timber, Trees, Woods	4, 6, 7, 8, 16, 20, 22, 24, 26, 29, 30, 31, 56, 65, 69, 73, 78, 80, 81, 93–109, 110, 111, 112, 113, 119, 120, 122, 128, 156, 161, 182, 185–199, 206, 211, 231
Wolves	20, 59–73, 93, 108, 122, 135, 203–212

PLACE-NAME INDEX

Abbey Hill 165
Alston 104
Anglezarke 3, 10, 20, 32, 104
Audley 104
Belmont 104
Black Combe 162
Black Coppice 30
Black Hill Lower 12
Black Hill Upper 12
Brant Rake 64
Brown Hill 12
Brown Rigg 68
Bryan Hey 104
Calf Hey 104
Cappanawalla 163
Churn Clough 104
Cold Within Hill 12
Counting Hill 12
Crosby Gill 68
Crowshaw Lodge 104
Darwen 120
Dean Clough 104
Delph Springs 104
Devoke Water 67, 68, 204
Dingle 104
Dunnerdale Beck 180
Earnsdale 104
Faierlokke 24
Fishmoor 104
Fox Bield 64
Gleninagh 163
Grange Brow 7

Gray Stone 64
Great Grassoms 162
Great Hill 12
Guide 104
Hall Beck 68
Hare Gill 64
Hempshaws 3, 10, 48
Hesk Fell 64
High Bullough 104
High Ground 68
High Rid 104
Hill Top 7
Hoar Stones Brow 28
Holden Wood 104
Hordern Stoops 14
Horwich 120
Hurst Hill 30
Jumbles 104
Ladder Crag 68
Lower Rivington 104
Mitchell's House 104
Moses Cocker's 47
Noon Hill Wood 6
Ogden 104
Old Rachel's 51
Parsonage 104
Pike How 68
Presbyterian Chapel 10
Rake Brook 104
Ravens Crag 180
Redmonds Edge 12
Ribble 119

Rishton 104
Roddlesworth 104
Rough Crag 68
Round Loaf 12
Sike Moss 68
Simms 48, 51
Spade Mill 104
Spitlers Edge 12
Standing Stones Hill 12
Storthes Gill 64
Stronstrey Bank 30
Sunnyhurst Hey 104
Swinside Fell 162
The Seat 68
Thwaites Fell 162
Turton & Entwistle 104

Turton Heights 7
Ulpha Fell 61, 62, 73, 210
Upper Rivington 104
Walves 104
Ward's 104
Water Crag 64, 68
Wayoh 104
White Coppice 3
White Ledge Hill 12
White Moss 64
White Wall 68
Will Narr 12, 24, 31
Winter Hill 24
Withnell 120
Worthington 104
Yarrow 9, 13, 15, 23, 31, 49, 55, 104

BIBLIOGRAPHY (2009-2014)

Books

Nimrod is lost in Orion and Osyris in the Doggestarre (2014)
Limnology (2012)
Moor Glisk (2012)
Field Notes, VOLUME ONE (2012)*
Landings (2009, 2010, 2011, 2012)

Booklets

I Know Not Where (2014)
Evidence of Capillary Beauty Dismantled (2013)
A List of Probable Flora (2013)*
Wolfhou (2013)*
Relics (2013)*
Bark, Xylem (2013)
Become a Ford (2013)
Rowk (2012)
Rill (2012)
Four Wing (2012)
Multitude (2012)
Domain (2012, 2014)
Ridgelines (2012)
Wolf Notes (2010, 2011)*
Into the Bare Moorland (2010)
Skin & Heather (2010)
Typography of the Shore (2009)*

* with Autumn Richardson

www.ingramcontent.com/pod-product-compliance
Lightning Source LLC
Chambersburg PA
CBHW070051080526
44586CB00013B/1007